I0813335

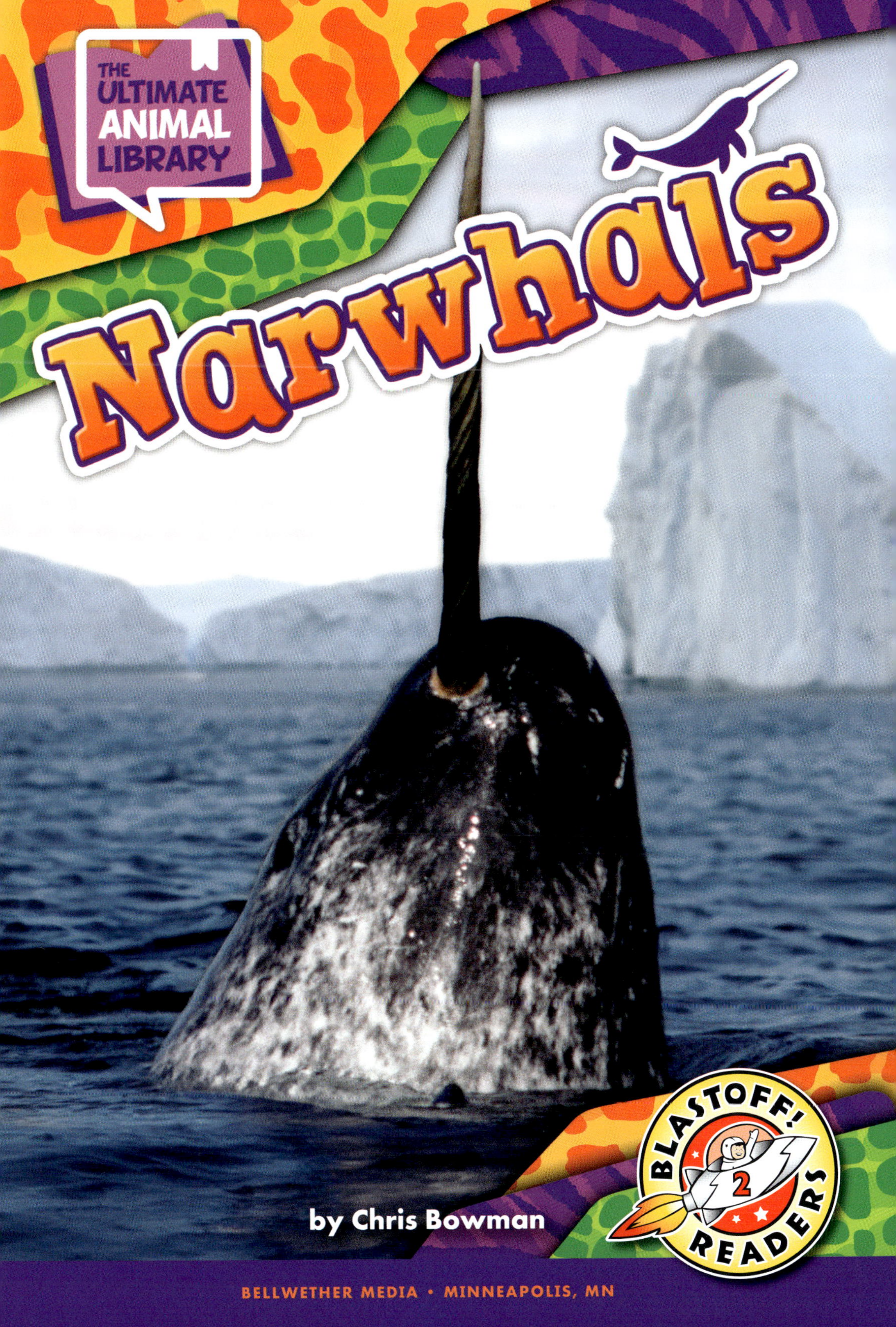
THE ULTIMATE ANIMAL LIBRARY
Narwhals
by Chris Bowman
BLASTOFF! 2 READERS
BELLWETHER MEDIA • MINNEAPOLIS, MN

Blastoff! Readers are carefully developed by literacy experts to build reading stamina and move students toward fluency by combining standards-based content with developmentally appropriate text.

Level 1 provides the most support through repetition of high-frequency words, light text, predictable sentence patterns, and strong visual support.

Level 2 offers early readers a bit more challenge through varied sentences, increased text load, and text-supportive special features.

Level 3 advances early-fluent readers toward fluency through increased text load, less reliance on photos, advancing concepts, longer sentences, and more complex special features.

Blastoff! Universe

Reading Level

Grade K

Grades 1–3

Grade 4

This edition first published in 2026 by Bellwether Media, Inc.

Library of Congress Cataloging-in-Publication Data

LC record for Narwhals available at: https://lccn.loc.gov/2025003964

Editor: Elizabeth Neuenfeldt Series Designer: Veah Demmin

Printed in the United States of America, North Mankato, MN.

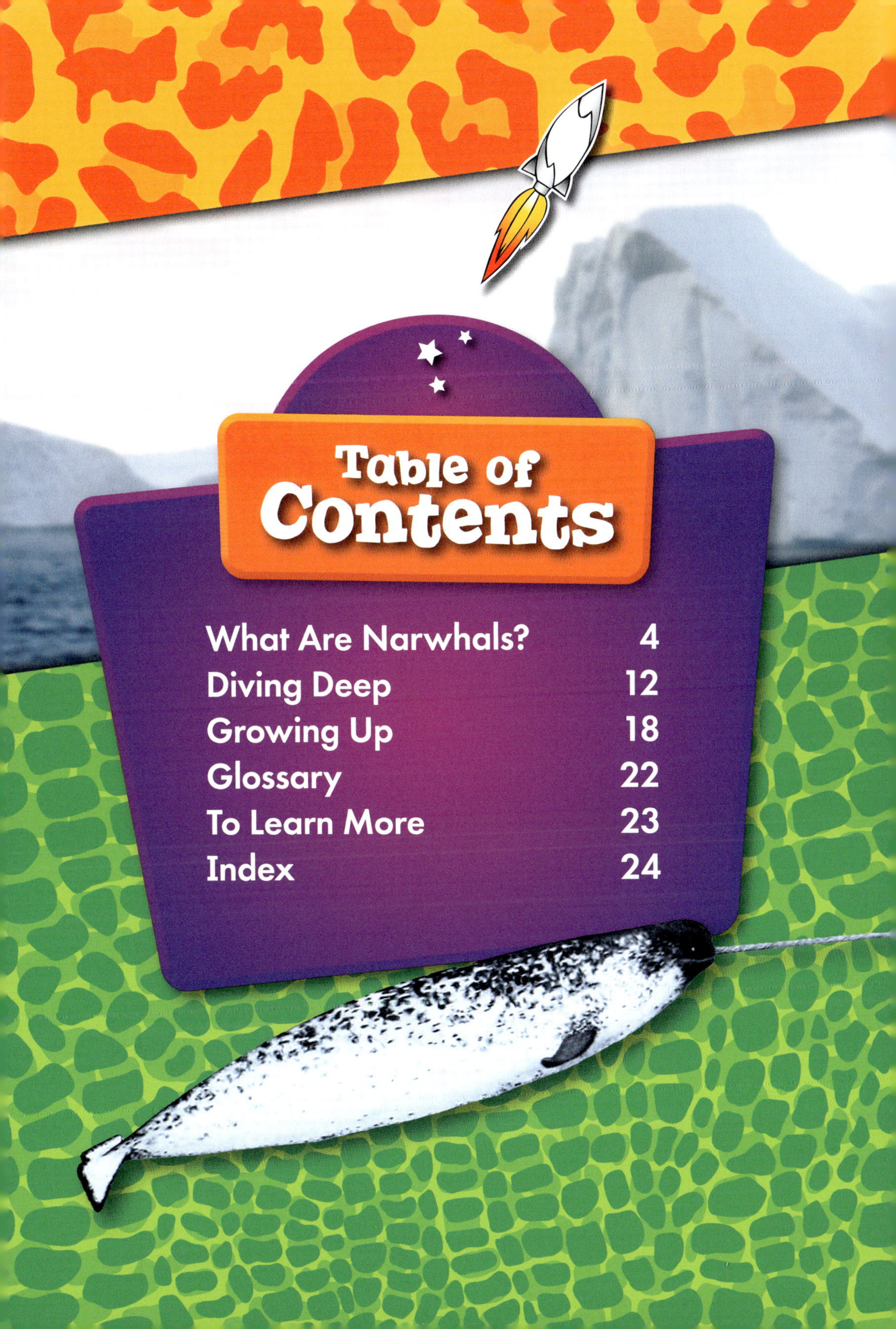

Table of Contents

What Are Narwhals?

Narwhals are whales. They live in **Arctic** waters. Males have a long **tusk**. It is actually a **spiraled** tooth! It can be 10 feet (3 meters) long.

Narwhal Report

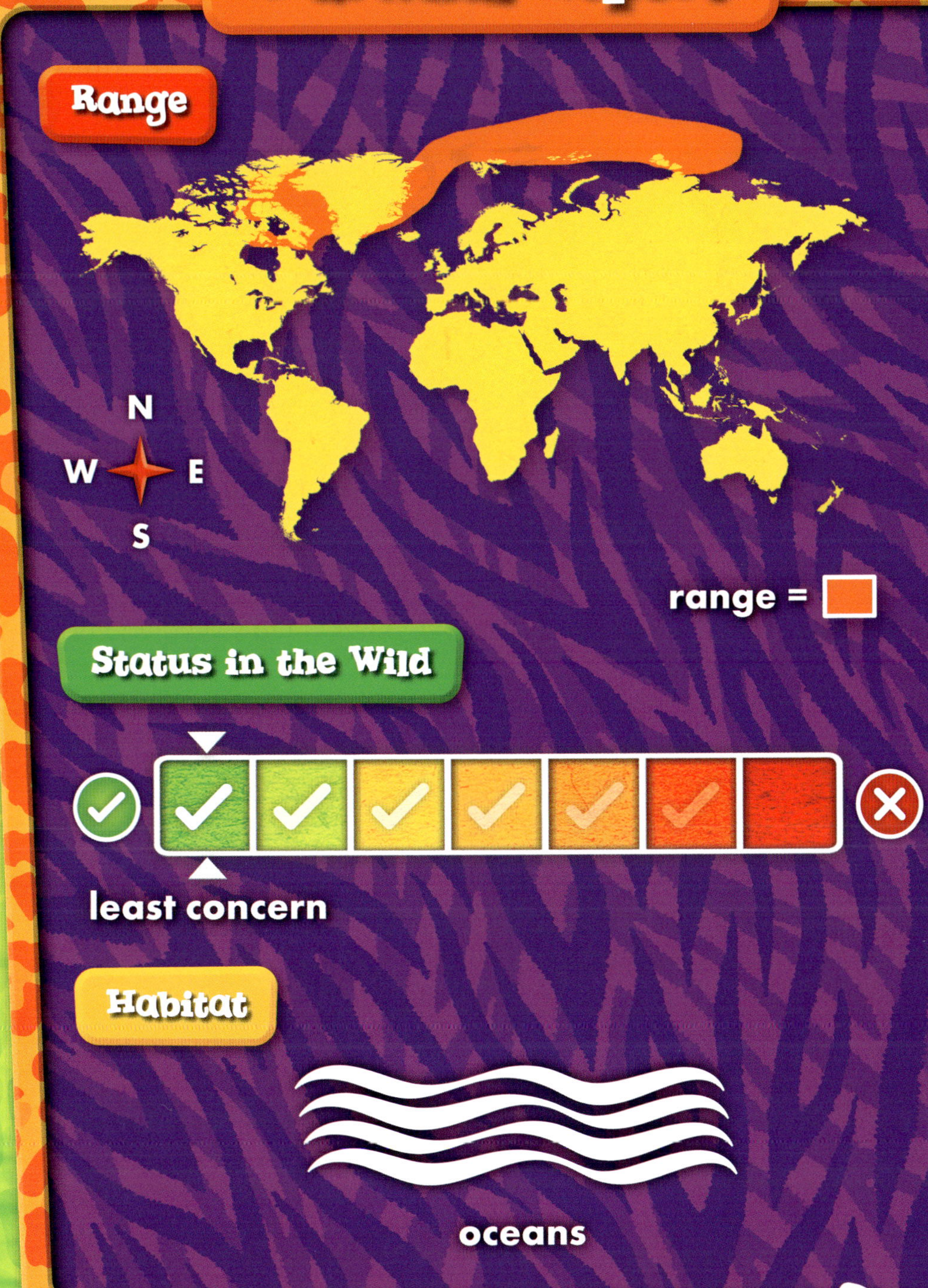

Narwhals are big.
They grow up to 18 feet
(5.5 meters) long!

Some weigh up to 4,200 pounds (1,905 kilograms).

Narwhals have spotted gray and white skin.

They are darker on the top.
Their bellies are white.

Narwhals have **blubber**. This keeps narwhals warm.

They breathe through a **blowhole** on their backs. They have small **flippers**.

blowhole
Spot a Narwhal
blowhole
tusk
flippers

Diving Deep

Narwhals swim in groups.
Groups are called **pods**.

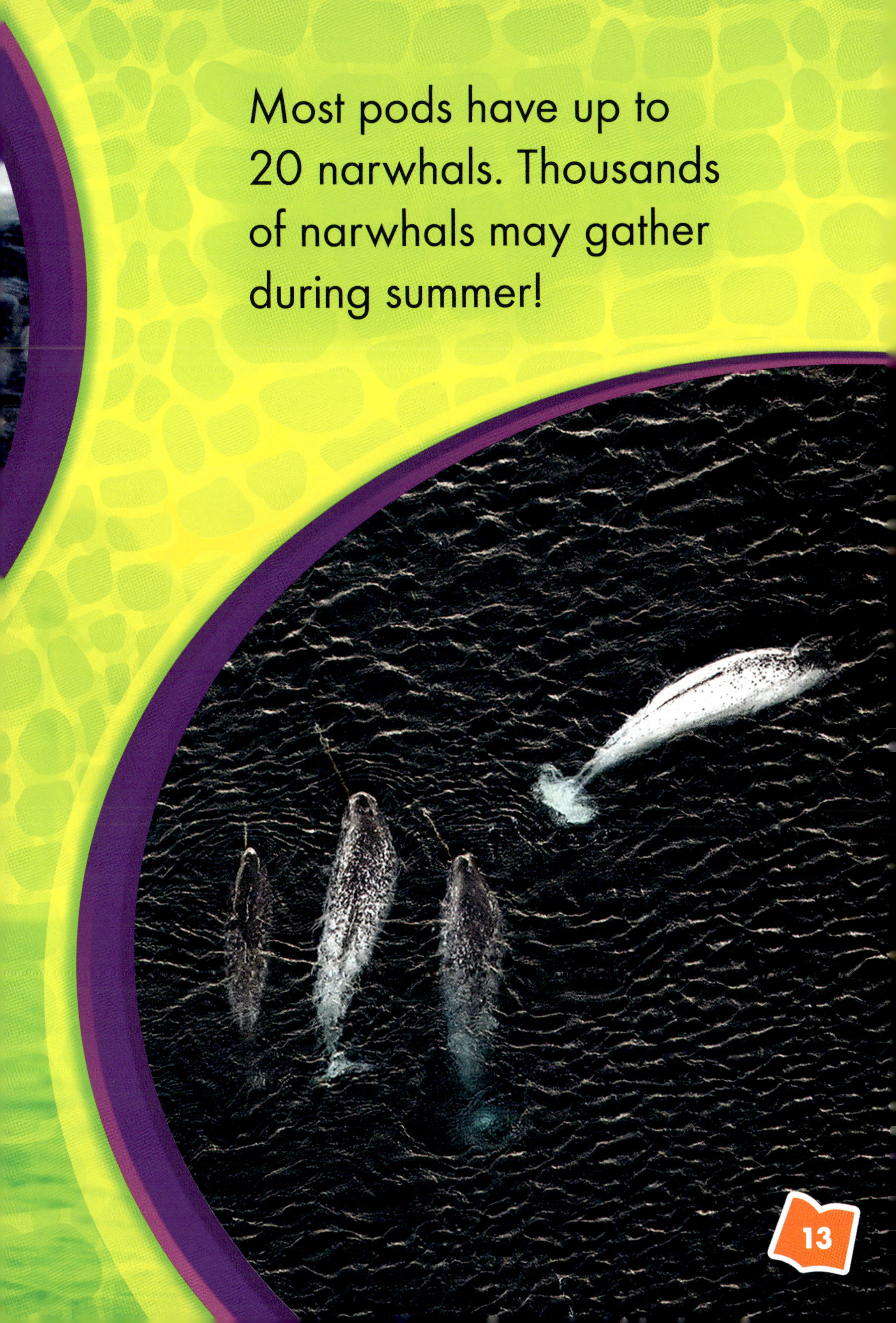

Most pods have up to 20 narwhals. Thousands of narwhals may gather during summer!

Narwhals swim to find food. They dive down to 5,900 feet (1,798 meters) deep!

They often eat fish and shrimp. They also eat squid.

Narwhals hide from **predators**. Orcas try to eat them.

Polar bears and walruses attack when narwhals come up for air.

Growing Up

Female narwhals are **pregnant** for about 14 months. They give birth to one **calf** in summer.

Calves are around 5 feet (1.5 meters) long. Their bodies are gray.

calf

Narwhal calves can swim right away. They **nurse** for at least one year.

Then they find food with their pod!

Life of a Narwhal

Name of Babies

calves

Number of Babies

1

Time Spent with Mom

at least 1 year

Life Span

up to 50 years

Glossary

Arctic—related to the cold, frozen land and seas around the North Pole

blowhole—the hole on top of a narwhal's head that is used for breathing

blubber—the layer of body fat that helps cold water animals stay warm

calf—a baby narwhal

flippers—wide, flat body parts that are used for swimming

nurse—to drink mom's milk

pods—groups of narwhals

predators—animals that hunt other animals for food

pregnant—carrying one or more unborn babies

spiraled—wound around something

tusk—the long, spiraled tooth of a narwhal

To Learn More

AT THE LIBRARY

Neuenfeldt, Elizabeth. *Arctic Animals*. Minneapolis, Minn.: Bellwether Media, 2023.

Rathburn, Betsy. *Narwhals*. Minneapolis, Minn.: Bellwether Media, 2021.

Schuh, Mari. *Narwhals*. Minneapolis, Minn.: Jump!, 2022.

ON THE WEB

FACTSURFER

Factsurfer.com gives you a safe, fun way to find more information.

1. Go to www.factsurfer.com.
2. Enter "narwhals" into the search box and click 🔍.
3. Select your book cover to see a list of related content.

Index

The images in this book are reproduced through the courtesy of: Superstock/ Flip Nicklin/ Minden Pictures, cover (narwhal), pp. 12, 18; Michal Balada, cover background, interior background; Alfmaler, cover (narwhal icon); NOAA United States National Marine Fisheries Service/ Wikipedia, p. 3; A & J Visage/ Alamy, pp. 4, 7, 10-11; Todd Mintz/ Alamy, pp. 6, 8, 9, 21; Doug Allan/ Nature Picture Library, p. 10; пресс-служба ПАО "Газпром нефть"/ Wikipedia, pp. 11, 13, 14-15; vaclav, p. 15 (polar bears); wildestanimal, p. 15 (orcas); by wildest animal/ Getty Images, pp. 15 (narwhal), 16, 23; Bjorn H Stuedal, p. 15 (walruses); Shawn Harper/ Hidden Ocean 2005 Expedition: NOAA Office of Ocean Exploration/ Wikipedia, p. 15 (fish); The Hidden Ocean, Arctic 2005 Exploration, NOAA-OE/ Wikipedia, p. 15 (squid); © 2004 by Tomasz Sienicki/ Wikipedia, p. 15 (shrimp); Paul Souders/ Alamy, p. 17; Superstock/ Animals Animals, pp. 18-19; Eric Baccega/ Minden Pictures, p. 20.